I've never written a foreword before for anyone, least of all an elflike cartoonist with guileless eyes, an ingratiating smile and a capacity for martinis that is astounding considering his size. Precisely why Hart requested this assignment from me is unknown. I rather think it's because I laugh at his jokes and about one third of the time I'm able to discern some .inner and hidden meanings in his wild woolly Left-Bank asides. It happens to be a fact that Johnny Hart is an unusual kind of guy and an unusual kind of humorist. His drawings and his wit can best be described as bold—and boldness is in short supply in the entertainment field nowadays. There are very few practicing humorists, cartoonists or authors who are willing to take an uncharted dip into a strange pool. To Mr. Hart's credit everlasting—he'll swim anywhere, wearing any kind of bathing suit.

To the uninitiated Hart reader, all this will seem pretty meaningless until you read and look at what he's written and drawn. To the Hart fan, this becomes somewhat redundant because you've already become familiar with his imaginative gremlin who makes you look at his pictures twice and reflect on his dialogue at least three times.

It all boils down to this: In the welter of ruttish, threadbare, third-hand humor that we're exposed to day after day, the freshness of Johnny Hart is an air-conditioning unit in a Bedouin tent on the Sahara. It feels good. And that's why I'm writing this foreword—as meaningless as it is—for nothing. So just don't sit there, Johnny Hart, with your leprechaun puss—go ahead and make me laugh!

Rod Serling

Also by the same author,
and available in Coronet Books:

Hey! B.C.
Hurray for B.C.
Back to B.C.

B.C.
Strikes Back

Johnny Hart

(ABRIDGED)

CORONET BOOKS
Hodder Fawcett Ltd., London

Copyright © 1961, 1962 by the New York
Herald Tribune, Inc.
Coronet Books edition 1971
Second impression 1972
Third impression 1973

This book is sold subject to the condition that
it shall not, by way of trade or otherwise, be
lent, re-sold, hired out or otherwise circulated
without the publisher's prior consent in any
form of binding or cover other than that in
which this is published and without a similar
condition including this condition being
imposed on the subsequent purchaser.

Printed and bound in Great Britain for
Coronet Books,
Hodder Fawcett Ltd,
St. Paul's House, Warwick Lane,
London, EC4P 4AH
by Hazell Watson & Viney Ltd,
Aylesbury, Bucks

ISBN 0 340 15679 1

TO A REAL SWEETHEART
OF A BROAD WHO HAS
SOMEHOW WEATHERED IT ALL;
TO MY MATE: BOBBY

THE BASEBALL IS MADE WITH THOUSANDS OF WINDINGS OF STRING.

HOW THE HECK DO YOU WIND STRING INTO A CUBE SHAPE?

SIMPLE. -- YOU USE A CUBE FOR THE CORE.

WHAT KIND OF CUBE DID YOU USE?

BOUILLON.

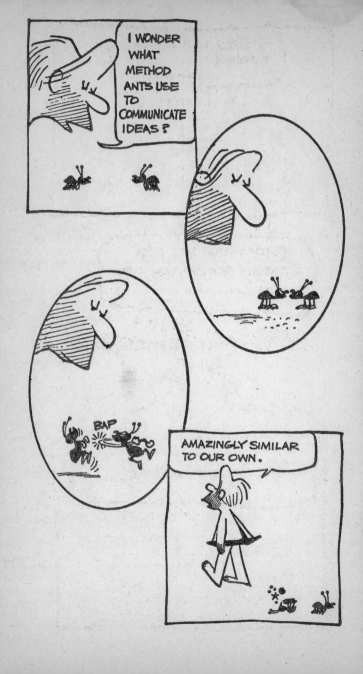

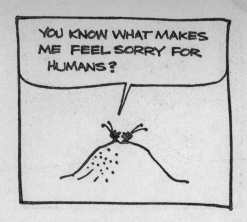

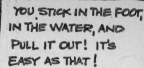

ONLY WILEY COULD SWIM THE DESERT.

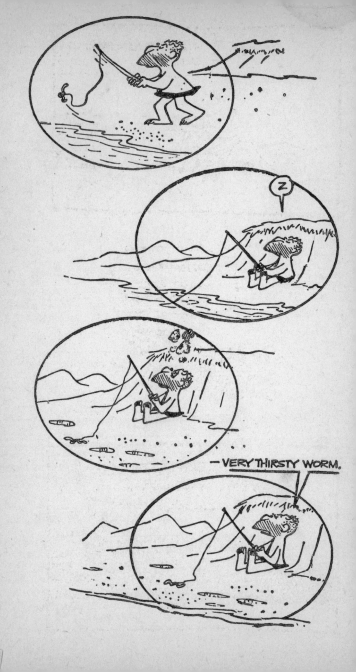

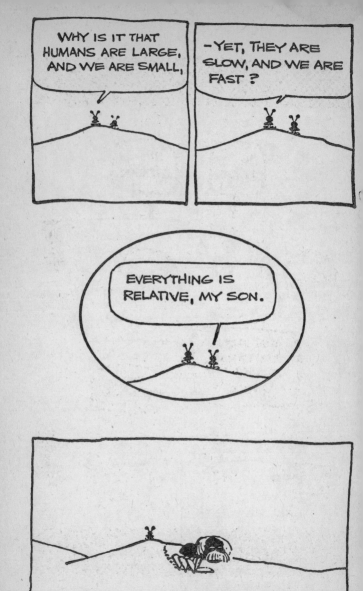

IT WAS INEVITABLE. SOMEBODY HAD TO INVENT SHAVING

WHOEVER IT IS, DOES A GREAT IMPERSONATION OF WILEY.

A HEART SHAPED FLOWER.

A GUY NEEDS THAT AT LEAST ONCE A YEAR.

I DON'T KNOW WHY WE DIDN'T THINK OF THIS BEFORE.

ZOT

ODD! I HAVE NO FEELING OF CANNIBALIZING AT ALL.

WHAT'S THAT?

I THOUGHT I HEARD SOMETHING! --LIKE HAIR GROWING!

YOU HEAR LOTS OF FUNNY THINGS AT NIGHT.

GOOD HEAVENS.

BALD, EH!

THIS IS AN INNOVATION IN LETTER WRITING: A "PYRAMID CLUB." PLEASE MAKE 3 DUPLICATES OF THIS LETTER AND MAIL THEM TO ME. —

FORWARD THE ORIGINAL TO A FRIEND AND ASK HIM TO DO LIKEWISE. A COMPLETE EXPLANATION WILL BE FORTHCOMING, PENDING A SUCCESSFUL OUTCOME.

THANK YOU,
WILEY.

AFTER A WHILE

HOW DID YOU EVER MAKE OUT WITH YOUR 'PYRAMID CLUB', WILEY?

GREAT.

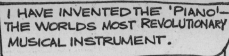

WHAT'S IT SOUND LIKE?

LIKE SOMEBODY BLOWING THROUGH A HOLE IN THE BACK OF A PIANO.

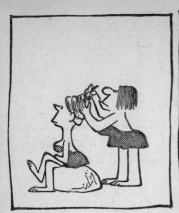

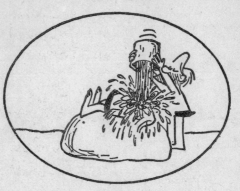

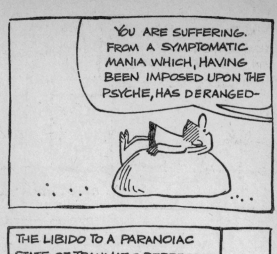

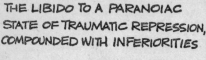

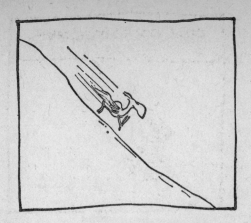

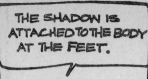

AAIEE!

I WONDER HOW COME YOUR FINGERS ONLY BEND DOWN?

DON'T BE SILLY. WHO'D WANT TO HOLD ANYTHING ON THE BACKS OF THEIR HANDS?

CRACK

DON'T KILL YOURSELF KID. IT'LL PROBABLY BURN OUT DURING RE-ENTRY.

UCLAN
NATO
GOP

NAACP

NASA-UN-
ASCAP

WCTU

DINOSAURS COULD RULE THE WORLD IF THEY COULD ORGANIZE THEIR SPEECH.